Bi.
Notebook

To

Happy Birthday

With love and best wishes from:

◇◇◇

5 January
Construction begins on the Golden Gate Bridge in
San Francisco.

_____

_____

_____

_____

_____

_____

_____

_____

_____

_____

_____

_____

_____

_____

1933 Birthday Notebook

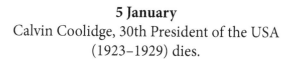

5 January
Calvin Coolidge, 30th President of the USA
(1923–1929) dies.

9 January

George Orwell's tramping memoir, *Down and Out in Paris and London*, is published.

◇◇◇

18 January
Botanist David Bellamy born.

30 January
Adolf Hitler is appointed as Chancellor of Germany.

_____

_____

_____

_____

_____

_____

_____

_____

_____

_____

_____

_____

_____

_____

1933 Birthday Notebook

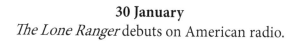

30 January
The Lone Ranger debuts on American radio.

1933 Birthday Notebook

31 January
Novelist John Galsworthy (*The Forsyte Saga*) dies aged 65.

9 February

The Oxford Union passes a resolution stating that 'this house will in no circumstances fight for its King and Country'.

1933 Birthday Notebook

15 February
Failed assassination attempt on Franklin D. Roosevelt, US President Elect.

1933 Birthday Notebook

17 February
The first edition of *Newsweek* magazine is published.

_____

_____

_____

_____

_____

_____

_____

_____

_____

_____

_____

_____

_____

_____

1933 Birthday Notebook

28 February
The first woman to serve in the US cabinet, Frances Perkins, is appointed Secretary of Labor.

_____

_____

_____

_____

_____

_____

_____

_____

_____

_____

_____

_____

_____

_____

1933 Birthday Notebook

2 March

The film *King Kong*, starring Fay Wray, premieres in the USA. It uses highly advanced special effects for its time.

_____

_____

_____

_____

_____

_____

_____

_____

_____

_____

_____

_____

_____

_____

_____

1933 Birthday Notebook

4 March

Franklin D. Roosevelt becomes the 32nd President of the United States.

_____

_____

_____

_____

_____

_____

_____

_____

_____

_____

_____

_____

_____

_____

_____

_____

1933 Birthday Notebook

◇◇

7 March
Elizabeth Magie and Charles Darrow invent the board game 'Monopoly' featuring the streets of Atlantic City, New Jersey.

_____

_____

_____

_____

_____

_____

_____

_____

_____

_____

_____

_____

_____

1933 Birthday Notebook

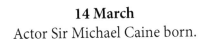

14 March
Actor Sir Michael Caine born.

1933 Birthday Notebook

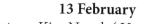

13 February
Actress Kim Novak (*Vertigo*) born.

_____

_____

_____

_____

_____

_____

_____

_____

_____

_____

_____

_____

_____

1933 Birthday Notebook

27 February
The German Reichstag is burnt down in suspicious circumstances, followed by a clampdown on civil liberties.

_____

_____

_____

_____

_____

_____

_____

_____

_____

_____

_____

_____

_____

_____

1933 Birthday Notebook

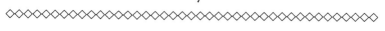

22 March
The first German concentration camp opens at Dachau.

27 March

Japan leaves the League of Nations, the forerunner of the
United Nations.

1933 Birthday Notebook

28 March
An Imperial Airways aeroplane crashes in Belgium, killing
15; the worst aviation disaster to that date.

_____

_____

_____

_____

_____

_____

_____

_____

_____

_____

_____

_____

_____

_____

1933 Birthday Notebook

2 April
English test cricketer Wally Hammond scores a record 336 runs against New Zealand.

1933 Birthday Notebook

3 April
Lieut. David McIntyre and Sir Douglas Douglas-Hamilton become the first men to fly over the summit of Everest.

_____

_____

_____

_____

_____

_____

_____

_____

_____

_____

_____

_____

_____

_____

4 April
The US airship *Akron* crashes off the coast of New Jersey,
killing 73 of its 76 crew.

_____

_____

_____

_____

_____

_____

_____

_____

_____

_____

_____

_____

_____

_____

1933 Birthday Notebook

16 April
Broadcaster Joan Bakewell (Baroness Bakewell) born.

1933 Birthday Notebook

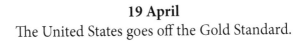

19 April
The United States goes off the Gold Standard.

22 April
Sir Henry Royce, co-founder of Rolls-Royce, dies aged 70.

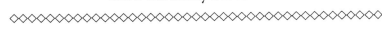

22 April
Francesco Agello sets a new world air speed record of 423.6 mph in a Macchi MC72 seaplane over Lake Garda, Italy.

_____

_____

_____

_____

_____

_____

_____

_____

_____

_____

_____

_____

_____

_____

26 April
The German secret police, the Gestapo, is established by
Hermann Göring.

1933 Birthday Notebook

30 April
Winifred Drinkwater becomes the first female commercial
pilot, flying planes for Midland and Scottish Air Ferries Ltd.

1933 Birthday Notebook

30 April
Country singer Willie Nelson born.

1933 Birthday Notebook

3 May
The parliament of the Irish Free State abolishes the Oath of Allegiance to the British crown.

1933 Birthday Notebook

8 May
Mahatma Gandhi begins a 21-day fast in protest over the
treatment of the 'untouchable' caste in India.

◇◇◇◇◇◇◇◇◇◇◇◇◇◇◇◇◇◇◇◇◇◇◇◇◇◇◇◇◇◇◇◇◇◇◇◇

10 May
Novelist Barbara Taylor-Bradford OBE
(*A Woman of Substance*) born.

_____

_____

_____

_____

_____

_____

_____

_____

_____

_____

_____

_____

_____

_____

1933 Birthday Notebook

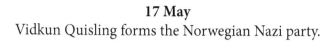

17 May
Vidkun Quisling forms the Norwegian Nazi party.

23 May
Actress Dame Joan Collins born.

1933 Birthday Notebook

27 May
The Chicago World's Fair opens.

_____

_____

_____

_____

_____

_____

_____

_____

_____

_____

_____

_____

_____

_____

1933 Birthday Notebook

27 May
Walt Disney's animated cartoon *The Three Little Pigs*
released.

1933 Birthday Notebook

16 June
The first drive-in movie theatre opens in Pennsauken
Township, near Camden, New Jersey.

◇◇

1 July
London's many bus, tube and tram companies are merged to form London Transport.

_____

_____

_____

_____

_____

_____

_____

_____

_____

_____

_____

_____

_____

_____

◇◇

22 July

Aviator Wiley Post becomes the first pilot to fly solo around the world, in 7 days 18 hours 45 minutes.

_____

_____

_____

_____

_____

_____

_____

_____

_____

_____

_____

_____

_____

26 July
Battersea Power Station in London begins operation.

1933 Birthday Notebook

◇◇

28 July
The first 'singing telegram' is delivered in the USA, to singer
and actor Rudy Vallee.

12 August
Winston Churchill makes his first speech warning of
German re-armament.

1933 Birthday Notebook

17 August
The Private Life of Henry VIII starring Charles Laughton is released. It becomes the first British film to win an Oscar.

_____

_____

_____

_____

_____

_____

_____

_____

_____

_____

_____

_____

_____

_____

4 September
General Batista seizes power in Cuba during a military coup.

1933 Birthday Notebook

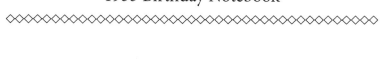

10 September
In the 53rd U.S. Men's Tennis National Championship: Fred
Perry beats Jack Crawford (6-3, 11-13, 4-6, 6-0, 6-1)

1933 Birthday Notebook

26 September
Notorious American gangster 'Machine Gun Kelly' is
arrested in Memphis, Tennessee.

_____

_____

_____

_____

_____

_____

_____

_____

_____

_____

_____

_____

_____

_____

1933 Birthday Notebook

◇◇

12 October

US army barracks on the island of Alcatraz are transferred to the Department of Justice to be turned into a prison.

_____

_____

_____

_____

_____

_____

_____

_____

_____

_____

_____

_____

_____

_____

12 October
Gangster John Dillinger escapes from jail in Allen County, Ohio, USA.

_____

_____

_____

_____

_____

_____

_____

_____

_____

_____

_____

_____

_____

_____

◇◇

14 October

Germany withdraws from the League of Nations.

_____

_____

_____

_____

_____

_____

_____

_____

_____

_____

_____

_____

_____

_____

1933 Birthday Notebook

17 October
Albert Einstein arrives in the United States as a refugee from Nazi Germany.

_____

_____

_____

_____

_____

_____

_____

_____

_____

_____

_____

_____

_____

1933 Birthday Notebook

24 October
London gangster twins Ronnie and Reggie Kray born (died 1995 and 2000).

_____

_____

_____

_____

_____

_____

_____

_____

_____

_____

_____

_____

_____

_____

11 November
The 'great black blizzard', the first 'dustbowl' storm, occurs across the Great Plains in the USA.

1933 Birthday Notebook

17 November
The Marx brothers film *Duck Soup* is released.

17 November
The USA formally recognises the USSR and begins trade deals between the two countries.

◇◇◇◇◇◇◇◇◇◇◇◇◇◇◇◇◇◇◇◇◇◇◇◇◇◇◇◇◇◇◇◇◇◇◇◇◇◇◇

22 November
Notorious gangsters 'Bonnie and Clyde' escape from a shoot-out with police near Sowers, Texas.

_____

_____

_____

_____

_____

_____

_____

_____

_____

_____

_____

_____

_____

_____

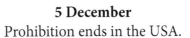

5 December
Prohibition ends in the USA.

_____

_____

_____

_____

_____

_____

_____

_____

_____

_____

_____

_____

_____

_____

_____

_____

_____

26 December

Patent for FM radio granted to inventor Edwin Howard Armstrong.

1933 Birthday Notebook

29 December
Ion Gheorghe Duca, Prime Minister of Romania, is
assassinated.

92870274R00035

Made in the USA
Lexington, KY
10 July 2018